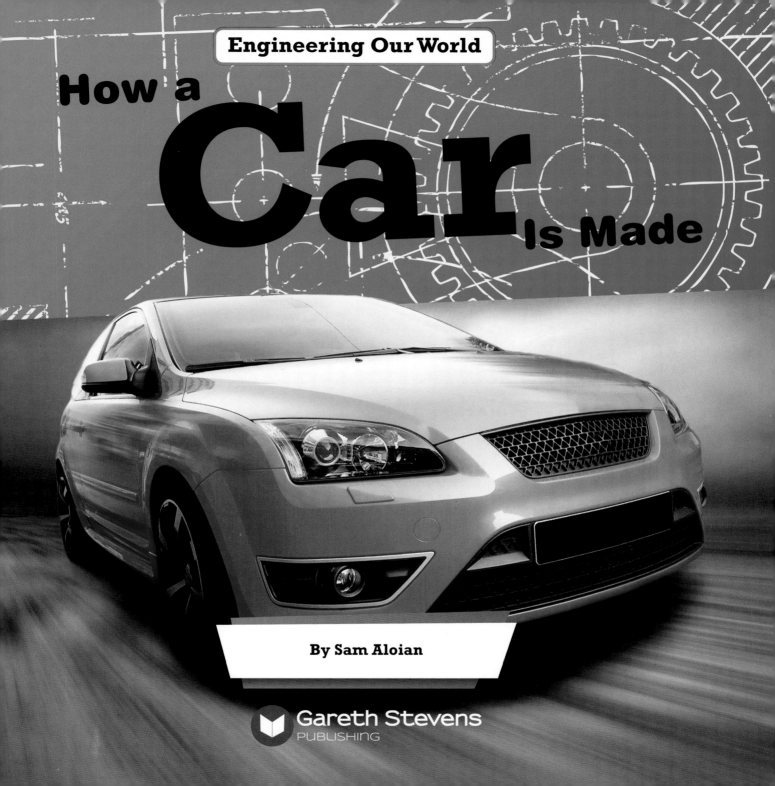

Engineering Our World

How a Car Is Made

By Sam Aloian

Gareth Stevens
PUBLISHING

Please visit our website, www.garethstevens.com. For a free color catalog of all our high-quality books, call toll free 1-800-542-2595 or fax 1-877-542-2596.

Library of Congress Cataloging-in-Publication Data

Aloian, Sam, author.
 How a car is made / Sam Aloian.
     pages cm. — (Engineering our world)
 Includes index.
ISBN 978-1-4824-3923-6 (pbk.)
ISBN 978-1-4824-3924-3 (6 pack)
ISBN 978-1-4824-3925-0 (library binding)
1. Automobiles—Design and construction—Juvenile literature. I. Title.
TL240.A434 2016
629.2'3—dc23

                                       2015031495

First Edition

Published in 2016 by
Gareth Stevens Publishing
111 East 14th Street, Suite 349
New York, NY 10003

Copyright © 2016 Gareth Stevens Publishing

Designer: Samantha DeMartin
Editor: Ryan Nagelhout

Photo credits: Cover, p. 1 Adrey Yurlov/Shutterstock.com; caption box stoonn/ Shutterstock.com; background Jason Winter/Shutterstock.com; p. 5 Yarygin/ Shutterstock.com; p. 7 (main) Omikron/Science Source/Getty Images; p. 7 (inset) Nataliya Hora/Shutterstock.com; p. 9 sorapol/Shutterstock.com; p. 11 safakcakir/Shutterstock.com; p. 13 Andrei Kholmov/Shutterstock.com; p. 15 Monty Rakusen/Cultura/Getty Images; p. 17 Bloomberg/Bloomberg/Getty Images; p. 19 Franz Marc Frei/LOOK-foto/LOOK/ Getty Images; p. 20 (bottle) Dan Kosmayer/Shutterstock.com; p. 20 (skewers) NRT/ Shutterstock.com; p. 20 (tape) Sean MacD/Shutterstock.com.

Printed in the United States of America

CPSIA compliance information: Batch #CS16GS: For further information contact Gareth Stevens, New York, New York at 1-800-542-2595.

Contents

Finding the Road 4

The Factory 6

Steel Shapes 8

Body Parts 10

Check and Paint 12

Parts and More Parts 14

On the Inside 16

Passing the Test 18

Make Your Own Car 20

Glossary 22

For More Information 23

Index 24

Words in the glossary appear in **bold** type the first time they are used in the text.

Finding the Road

Cars, trucks, and vans are all different kinds of **motor vehicles**. They help us get from place to place, making travel easier for millions of people. But what are cars made of? And where do they come from?

Cars are amazing machines that are filled with lots of **technology**, but we use equally amazing machines to make them. Let's see how the ideas of yesterday are paired with the technology of today to make our cars!

Building Blocks

Workers called engineers **design** cars. They figure out how each model looks on the outside and what features, called options, the car has inside. They make cars look cool and make sure they're safe for us to ride in!

The first cars were often called "horseless carriages" because they looked like the wagons commonly pulled by horses, but used electric or gas engines instead of horses!

The Factory

Today, cars are made in factories. One of the earliest factories was set up by the Ford Motor Company for its Model A car. One person would work on a station with all the parts needed to build a single car.

Cars today are made using a moving **assembly** line. On a moving assembly line, cars are put together piece by piece. Workers stay in one place, adding a certain part to each car as the car rolls through the factory.

Building Blocks

Henry Ford is commonly thought to have invented the moving assembly line, but Ransom E. Olds used an assembly line to make the Oldsmobile Curved Dash as early as 1901!

Henry Ford's Model T was another early assembly-line vehicle. Ford sold more than 15 million Model Ts between 1908 and 1927

modern moving assembly line

early moving assembly line

Steel Shapes

Today's cars are made from giant rolls of a strong metal called steel. The steel is unrolled flat, then pressed by 5,000-ton (4,536 mt) machines that **squeeze** these steel rolls into pieces that can be shaped using **molds**.

These molds are also called dies. Each die has top and bottom pieces that push on the steel to bend it into shape. The dies are very heavy and are used to mold steel over and over again.

Building Blocks

Assembly lines in giant factories can stretch very long distances. Ford's Michigan Assembly Plant is 3 miles (4.8 km) long and can make five different kinds of cars!

Each plant has thousands of dies to make car parts. Some factories are called stamping plants and use their many dies to make parts used in other factories.

Body Parts

The stamped parts are moved to the body shop, where car assembly begins. The main body of the car, called the frame, is set up there. The door, floor, and roof panels are put into position.

These steel parts are **welded** together using machines that heat pieces of metal quickly until they melt. The metal then hardens together as one, connecting pieces to make them stronger. Welding machines have arms that move around the car quickly to weld pieces into place.

Building Blocks

Welding was once done by hand. Today, machines on each side of the assembly line quickly weld the car together.

Welding machines add welds about 1 to 2 inches (2.5 to 5 cm) apart to connect metal pieces together.

Check and Paint

A line of welding machines continues to add parts to the car as it moves along the line. Parts for the back of the car, called the trunk, are added along with the car's fenders. The fenders go on the front and back of cars to protect the vehicle if something runs into it.

Once the outer body of the car is assembled and checked for **quality**, it's ready for paint. At least three coats of paint are added to the body before it leaves the paint shop.

Building Blocks

Many car models have a few different paint colors that customers can pick from. Some more expensive cars get their final color picked by customers before being painted.

Quality checks make sure the car's body parts line up and were added correctly. You wouldn't want a fender falling off when you drive!

Parts and More Parts

Once the body paint dries, a car is moved to the parts-assembly area of the factory. This is where the car's systems are added to the body.

The main power source in a car is its engine. The **transmission** helps that power actually move the car, while the suspension system connects the body of the car to the wheels that touch the roadway.

All these systems are added during parts assembly. Workers using cranes lower the body onto the engine, transmission, and suspension systems.

Building Blocks

Between 3,000 and 4,000 parts are added to a car during assembly. There are thousands more parts in a car if you count the screws and bolts needed to keep it all together!

Autoworkers often work in pairs to mount a car's parts to the body. Working together they quickly move around pieces that are heavy or hard to handle.

On the Inside

As the car keeps moving through the factory, wheels are added to the suspension system. Special glass windows are added to finish the car's outer assembly.

Next, the inside of the car is finished. Carpets are added to the floor. The dashboard and steering wheel are added, too. Robots add seats and other parts that make up the car's interior. Workers add other things like radios and even TVs! When the interior is finished, the car's construction is complete.

Building Blocks

Workers also add the **fluids** that keep a car running. Motor oil, brake oil, and even wiper fluid go in the car so workers can make sure there aren't any leaks!

People and machines work together in a car factory to build vehicles quickly. The robots do work that could be dangerous, while people do **delicate** tasks robots can't complete.

Passing the Test

Once the car is fully assembled, it's tested to make sure it's ready for the road. The engine and other systems are checked, and the parts under the car are tested. The car is driven by workers to make sure everything inside is ready, too.

Very bright lights are shined on the paint job to make sure there aren't any **scratches** or mistakes. Once the car is ready, it's shipped off to a customer or to a **car dealership** to wait for an owner!

Building Blocks

Volkswagen has a factory in downtown Dresden, Germany, that's transparent, or see-through. You can visit the factory and watch through glass walls as their cars get built!

Car parts are brought to Volkswagen's Dresden factory using the same railroad tracks people travel on throughout the city!

Make Your Own Car

Now that you know the basics of building a vehicle, here's how you can make your own balloon-powered car.

What You Need:

- balloon
- bottle caps
- water bottle
- 4 straws
- tape
- 2 wooden skewers

How to:

1. tape 2 straws to bottom of water bottle

2. insert skewers into straws

3. poke holes in bottle caps

4. stick bottle caps on wooden skewers

5. tape balloon to other 2 straws

6. poke hole in top of bottle

7. insert straws through top hole and bottle opening

8. blow up balloon through straws and let go!

Glossary

assembly: the act of building a complete object from parts

car dealership: a place that shows off and sells new and used cars

delicate: easily broken or upset

design: to create the pattern or shape of something

fluid: matter able to flow or take the shape of a container

mold: the frame on, around, or in which something is shaped

motor vehicle: an automobile

quality: the grade or makeup of something

scratch: a mark made by something sharp

squeeze: to press together

technology: the way people do something using tools and the tools that they use

transmission: the gears that carry power from the engine to the wheels that drive the car

weld: to join pieces of metal by heating and allowing the edges to flow together

For More Information

Books

Economy, Peter. *New Car Design*. Novato, CA: Treasure Bay, 2010.

Hammelef, Danielle S. *Building a Car*. North Mankato, MN: Capstone Press, 2014.

Stamps, Caroline. *Cars*. New York, NY: DK Publishing, 2013.

Websites

Create a Car
abcya.com/create_and_build_car.htm
This interactive website lets you create your own car in an online factory.

How Are Cars Made?
www.toyota.co.jp/en/kids/car
Find out more about how cars are designed and built at this Toyota website.

Index

body 10, 12, 13, 14, 15

body shop 10

carpets 16

dashboard 16

dies 8, 9

engineers 4

engines 5, 14, 18

fenders 12, 13

fluids 16

frame 10

molds 8

moving assembly line 6, 7, 8

paint 12, 14, 18

parts assembly 14

quality checks 12, 13

radios 16

robots 16, 17

seats 16

stamping plants 9

steel 8, 10

steering wheel 16

suspension system 14, 16

technology 4

tests 18

transmission 14

trunk 12

TVs 16

welding machines 10, 11, 12

wheels 14, 16

windows 16